F I

CW00525636

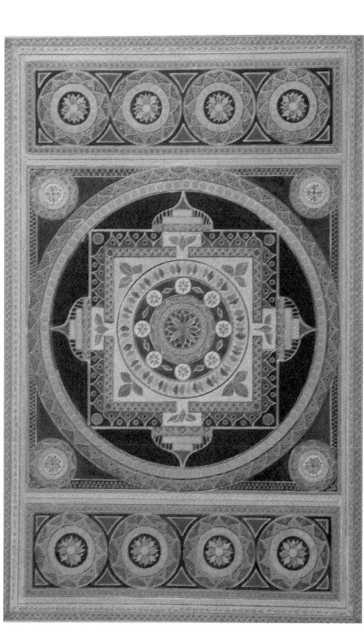

Fifty-Six Poems

by

Pete Gage

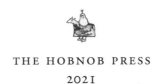

THE HOBNOB PRESS

2021

First published in the United Kingdom in 2021

by The Hobnob Press,
8 Lock Warehouse, Severn Road, Gloucester GL1 2GA
www.hobnobpress.co.uk

© Pete Gage text and images, 2021

British Library Cataloguing in Publication Data
A catalogue record for this book is available from the British Library

ISBN 978-1-914407-12-3

Typeset in Adobe Garamond Pro 12/14 pt.
Typesetting and origination by John Chandler

To the Memory of
Rose Hannah Florence Gage

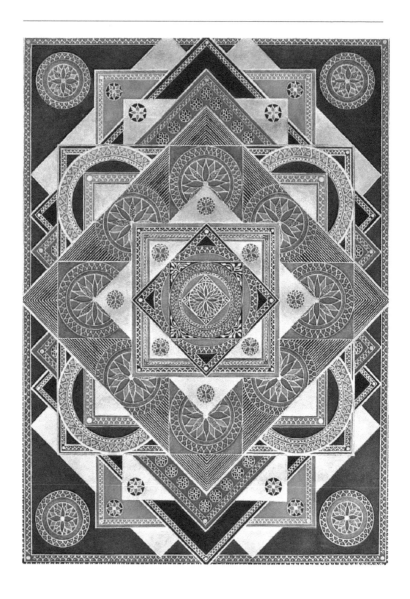

Who is it ambles across this page
in time to a cricket call,
or blackbird song soaring over above
the impetuous roar of the Avoncliff weir?

Is it he, there, in the pollenated air,
calling from afar on that fruitful shore?
Is it a youth who calls in the midsummer heat,
or an old man who has journeyed far?

Someone sits by the water and mourns
in the waist-deep summer
for the moments he missed.
Another lies in the warmth of the sun,
in the tall grass that belongs to the sky,
he whose senses absorb at last
the essence from where he's come.

And who is it ambles through this summer's day
as I do across this page?
Is it he who has always been here, like now,
or I who have come of age?

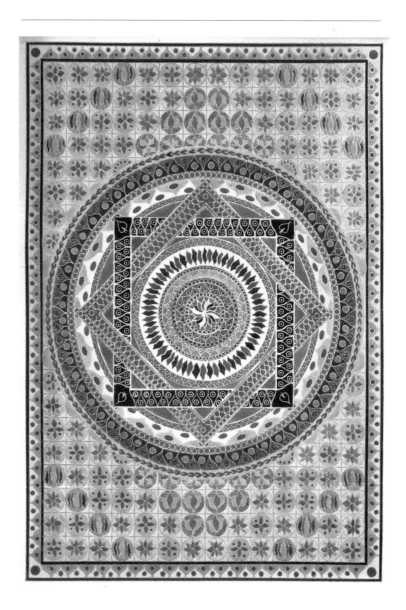

I walked along today with Robert Schumann;
passed through air and spaces where he breathed;
perhaps I even stood where he had pondered
on a day when he had peace and harmony.

A Florestan or spirit of Eusebius
may well have breezed around us in the room;
the atmosphere was cool and quietly murmured
those sounds we hear when we are most alone.

I heard the final pages of his Manfred,
and Trio Number Three's first wistful tune;
I felt the rush of all his joyous musings,
and the melancholy moaning of his gloom.

I lingered for as long as it was fitting,
next to the age-ing keyboard that he played
in those days of fleeting sanity and ramblings;
I caressed embroidered covers Clara made.

I saw the locks of hair of these two lovers,
and I longed to touch them both in their embrace.
I saw their love dissected in their letters,
notes on fading parchment in the case.

And when I'd caught my breath I sat in silence
to realise that this was more than he;
it was a channel through whose sacred earthly karma
we are gifted with his timeless legacy.

A taxi lay in waiting by the Schumannhaus;
I was swept from those sad heights down to the ground;
into Bonn we drove, and I was grateful;
and tearful, though I did not make a sound.

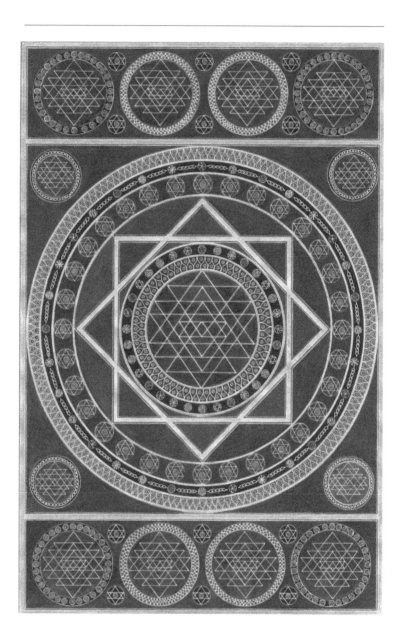

Safely rooted on that island, simple lifetime love now
   blooming,
you at peace on our sofa sighing, with your curling spine,
while I wander endlessly route-ing
nameless countries, none are mine.

Crazed by days' repeating journeys, all in steady planned
      manoeuvre,
unprotected by your murmur, in foreign pristine sheets I lie,
you fulfiling sampled pleasures,
attending to our young, pacify.

I would never take them from you, neither worldly joys nor
      heaven.
With inner strength you built a rhythm,
as pulse to your life, now quite renewed.

You upon that island finding separation bodes you well,
as you relish green and pleasant, mother nature's nurtured
      blessing,
I am exiled, endless journey,
far-off lands, unimpressing.

Abroad this daylight, eyes all-seeing, heart remorseful,
      distant being,
open channels, notwithstanding, you and individual I
are soon repairing, breaking habits
once that caused our love to sigh.

I would never take it from you, quiet dignity rekindled;
significantly you've stumbled upon your island,
as though inrending so to do.

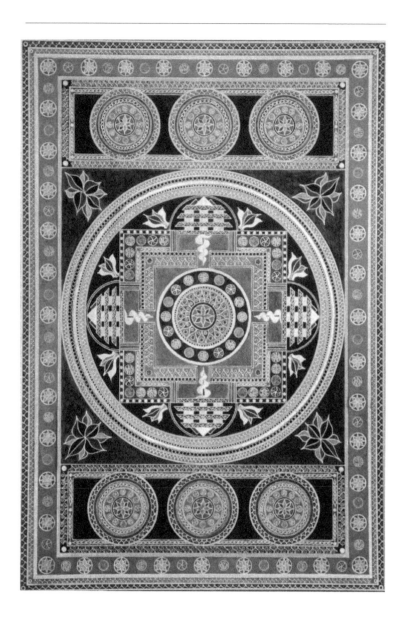

You are in my sights,
as a bird who is free in a field;
as the wings are in full flight
so my heart has come to feel.

You are in my grasp,
as a bird who comes to rest
in my hand, who leaves as fast
to return to its warm nest.

You are in my heart,
as a bird within a shell;
a bird who, though departs,
comes back to me as well.

And this is what he needs,
though a man who is full-grown,
whose fledglings he has loved,
whose feelings he has known.

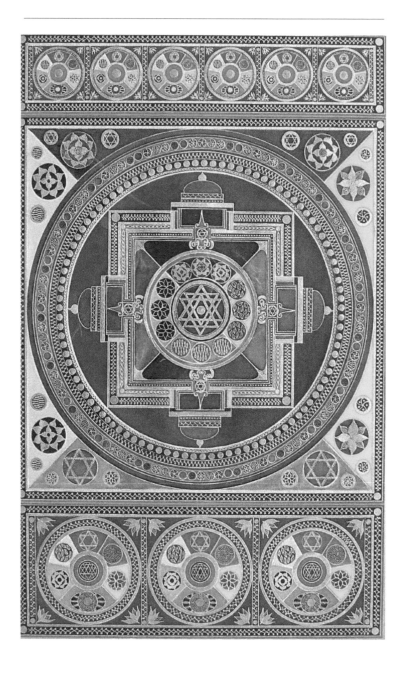

Beside me in this strange room
I have spread out my offerings;
credentials, the homely devices to which I cling,
all in their respective order.
Books to sense acheivement in surrender,
music to re-enforce a spiritual path,
a clock telling not so much the time,
as a useful mantra substitute;
one that I can meditate upon.
There are books that teach eradication,
compassion and other musings of the Buddha;
while reflections of my fellowship remind me
of my dependencies, our threat to one another.
Checking every page I turn,
my eyes get weary, and I raise them in despair.
They rest upon two pictures that I carry:
two jewels that shine more brightly than the rest.

Off-spring, gentle children turning into women,
remind me there is love and care in my life;
Though I'm alone within these walls I hear their laughter;
the daughters in the photographs are mine.
I allow myself these ample consolations;
my simple sights to soothe me and to heal;
once I'd weep as distance cut right through me,
but self-pity has at long-last had its day.

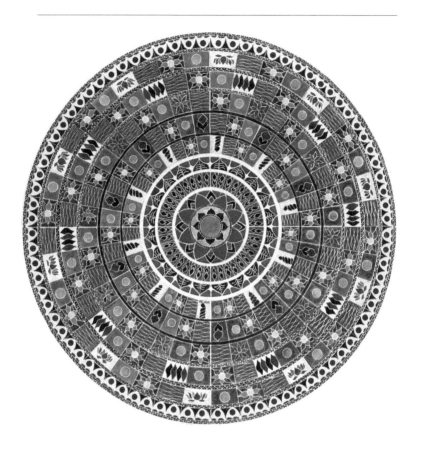

On the road recalling recent travellings;
journeying into untouched lands
where I'll shed emotion's cloak,
then languish in my solitude
til the light breaks through
into my darkened soul.
Remembering the body's rush
in response to the crazy crowd,
my uncontrolled surrender to the heart's moment:
murmuring of its own volition through my larynx,
release through a groaning ecstasy,
opening the channels from the root to the crown.
I can feel those wheels now,
churning through the debris
as I look out
through tired eyes
at the road
my heart
has chosen.

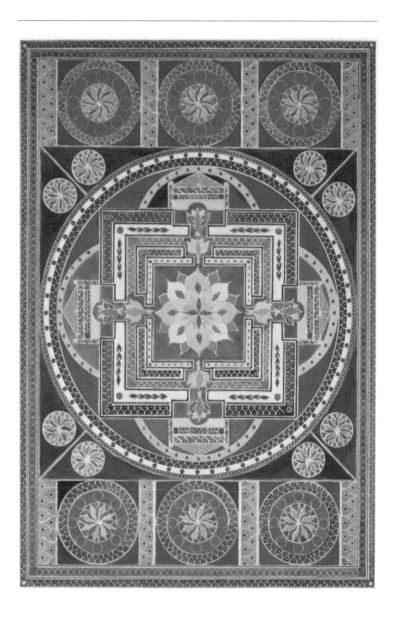

L ove, you there, lying on our bed,
embedded there soft against the air,
without my warmth,
nor thought of me in sleep,
dreaming unaware
with such instinctive flair, remember what I said:

Less there'll be of love for us,
as unloved here I taste a tear;
without your body close,
I sleeplessly dream of you;
sensing you so near to me,
I'll scatter fear and sorrow, and rise above.

Love, soft skin to tender touch,
untouched head upon our ruffled bed,
without our tender kiss,
or tangled arms in sleep.
Remember what I said.
I'll ache for you instead,
and miss you much too much.

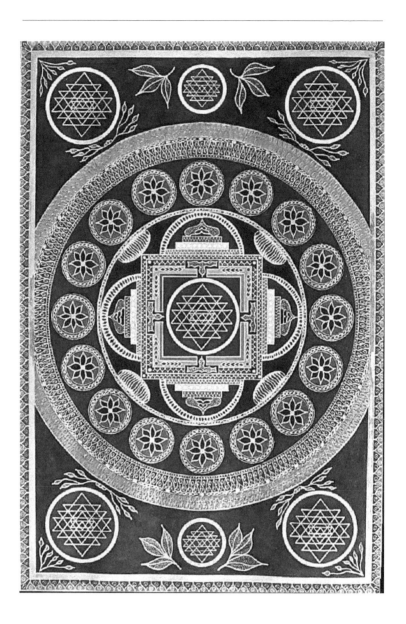

Wide-winged, the echo of my song glides in,
  descending to earth,
returns to find its way,
re-tracing steps to birth,
its lyric born of notion, whim;
the silent interim,
stripped of flesh,
beyond the bone;
its tissue just a murmur;
a tone whose chords eternal winds inspire;
its song surrounding voicelessness,
joins the internal choir.

My ears no longer bend to hear
these breezes once caressed;
against a wall of formlessness,
their echoes disappear.
This song we once inhabited,
dissolves in its own space.
Not into air, not fire, nor water-bound;
but to earth itself this sound now fades
with neither fate nor trace.

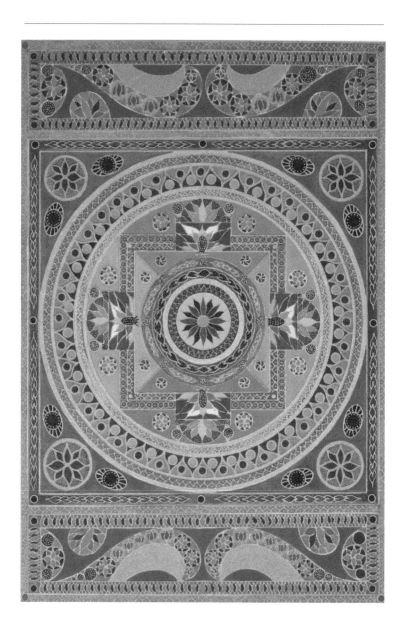

Here, with head that clears;
a clearing head,
not like heads that cleared
when lost or smeared;
instead this head
gives space and air
to grace, and care
to thought, and clarity.

Once, an aching heart;
a heart that ached,
a numbing ache of heart
whose poundings start
to break; this ache
outlives its reign
and gives the pain
up to reality.

Now, a soul that breathes;
a breathing soul,
my singing soul that breathes;
not lost nor cold,
but whole; this soul
instead has part
of head and heart
wrapped up in sanity.

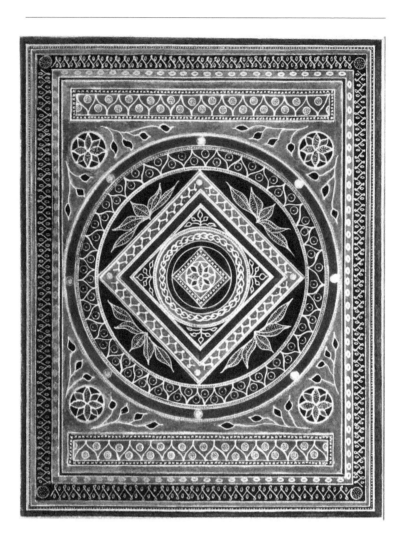

This brittle air bites,
    windlessly breathes and excites;
the chill will penetrate,
and leave at will,
challenging the land
to survive in tact.

This icy mist cools to freeze
a paradise of lakes and trees
in lines of white shadow,
high and bright upon the eye;
a blinding, shining light.

This fair and fickle sight,
across whose glacier,
night will fall
and mesmerise or mimic death,
freezing the breath
and blistering the eyes.

Out there,
my own dry world flakes like snow,
unfurled in the storms of my despair;
I shiver at my fate,
expecting neither love nor hate
to enter there.

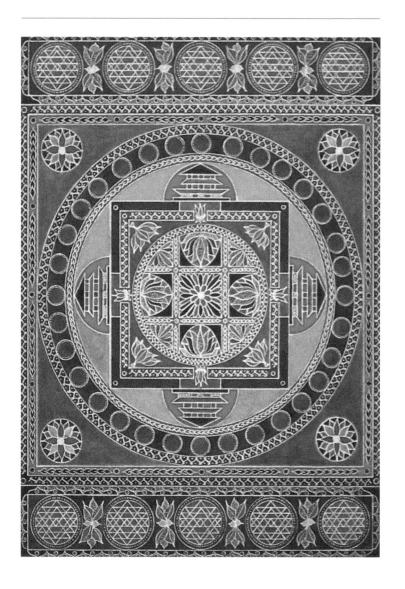

Within me pounding, nerve ends sounding
the heart's abounding song in flight;
whilst out there burning, spirit discerning
what is wrong from what is right.

But who's deciding? Over-riding
thought has power to invent
a choice of being, never seeing
past religious sacrament.

Before, confusing issues, choosing
toil over sweet content.
Constant striving and conniving
to appease ambition's temperament.

But now, without concealing truth, revealing
all originality;
no pious praying, no word decaying
the pure reality.

Without this burning ego yearning
for illusions to substantiate,
there is a dying to all this trying
to establish or create.

Quietly attending, I watch unending
thought; it weaves and vies for power;
ah! but with passive seeing, enlightened being,
much like the wind or a flower.

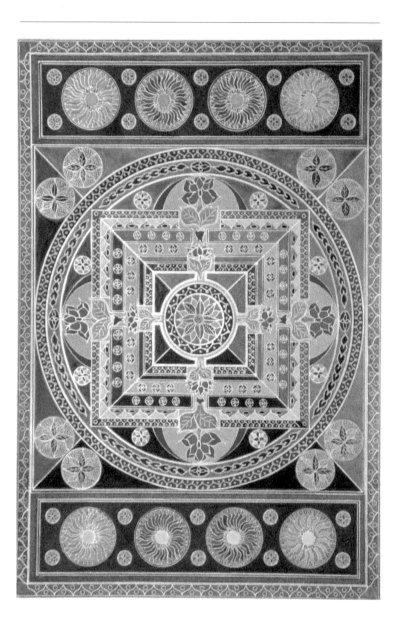

L ight heart, head light-hearted,
journey's end where journeys started;
evolving, world unending space,
warning creed and race
to recognise, but not to choose,
nor turn away by chance to lose.

From the dark, this darkened insight
now reveals its senses, spotlight
on the winds within through chakra spinning;
enlightenment with no beginning;
not a path nor door to enter,
not with edges, nor with centre.

Within the heart, cells multiplying,
pulse reminding, time denying;
no notion, word or thought invents
identity for a seventh sense;
the tune that cuts the silence brings
eternity to these imaginings.

In the light, the heart's light
directed outward, once undetected,
now caught by the passing time;
enchanted by the bliss of perfection granted.
I'm still clinging to earthly matters,
but my heart is wildly singing to heaven.

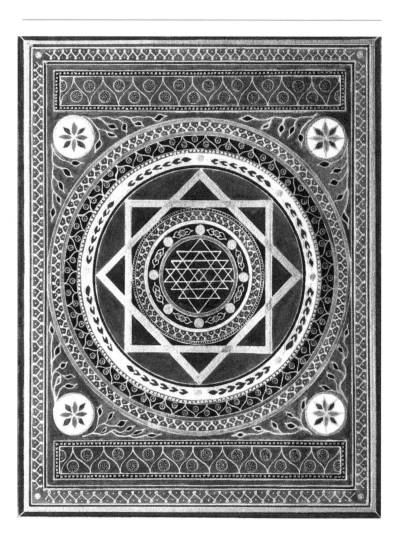

This alliance limps through the ruins of its avenues;
we are clinging like bats to vows created
in a desperate plea for sanctuary;
these weary bones buckle on weakened ankles,
ever fearful of the exile separation offers.
Our footing falters on the crumbling path
etched in the name of purpose,
procreation and protection;
and our eyes only meet through tears that mingle,
shed for our dependency in momentary surrender.

Hands and arms that once our souls reached out for
give way in the heat of our exposure;
the faces of our inner child
reveal a pain so long concealed;
our one spirit broken,
looking out onto a desolate field,
the fire of our defences burned to the quick
in this, our stark reality.

True to self, but blindly on,
a dying habit leads us,
seduced by a familiar safety.
Rising from the smoke,
a sign not of the senses, beckons,
giving us neither clue nor reason why.
Stripped of all intention,
refugees of respectability,
we question, shall we follow?
And we follow still unable
to let go our trembling hands.

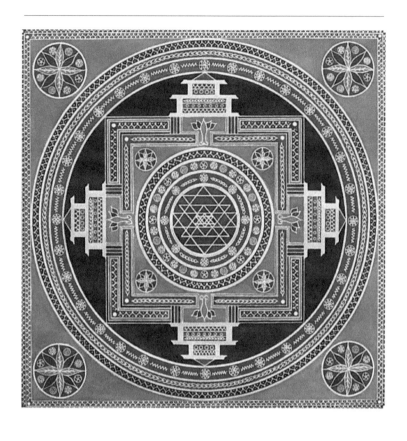

Something gentle rubs against my heart,
if heart's this feeling thing I cannot trace;
nor does it have a place to stay,
it wants a home, but never shows its face.

Something bitter tastes divine to me,
though not a taste I savour with the tongue;
a taste that all-pervades my being,
and whets my failing appetite 'til done.

Something in the senses lets me know;
but through which channel I could never say;
its message, though my intellect can't hear,
has meaning such that words cannot portray.

Something moves me such though I lay still;
and in the stillness breathes the thing I mean;
but I can only trust it lives within,
for when I look it's nowhere to be seen.

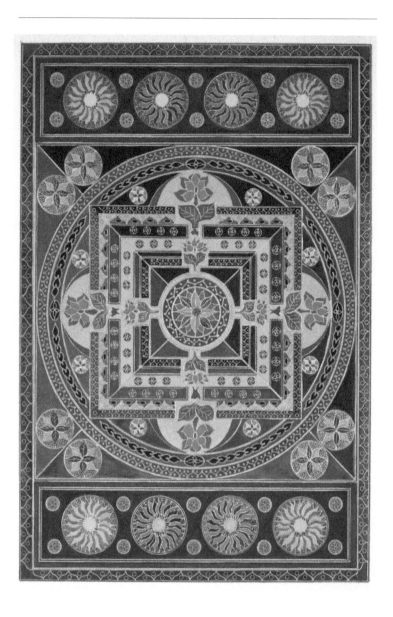

Without you here,
wild flowers go unnoticed.
The rain lingers on
like the tear on your cheek,
and the quiet air,
heavy with our parting,
hangs on like mist
for your return.

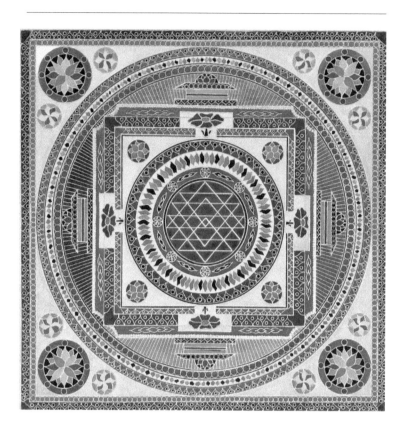

I rolled, arriving into being,
as rain that collects on the sand.
Tumbling like mercury down those arid slopes,
I landed on thirsty soil
laden with carefully chosen fruits,
just enough for today,
while the paths of tomorrow lay uncharted,
and the past hung on like the lifeless limb
of a weeping willow.
I laid my head upon the shoulders
of sympathetic ghosts,
looking back on old ideas of freedom
and dreams of nirvana
laughing at the images they formed.
I have no fear of imperfection.

All is quiet and clear.
Whatever would have once
destroyed my chance of heaven,
was severed on my former battlefields.
A clean cut left the slither of a scar;
I wear it without pride or consolation.
The soldier in me, once so barely visible
through the mist of those old cravings,
has returned as must his forbears once have done,
feet now firmly rooted, and not sinking in the sand.
Slowly the wheels of circumstance turn,
to deny humiliation for my slowly fading man.

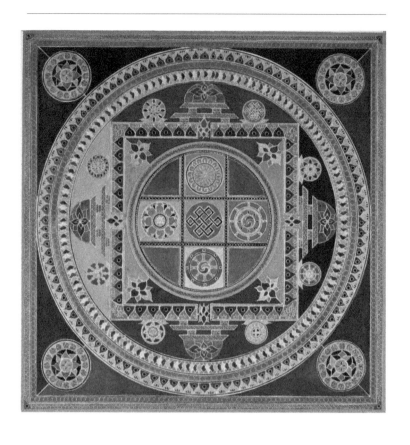

This could be the room
where once I grieved my losses;
losses of all that passed
in the bleak days of yearning.
This room could be the one
I'd toss and turn in,
absorbing every stifled blow
from the hunger of my learning.
This room could be from
time back then, when I was cold,
alone like now, and unprepared,
without the warmth and safety
of experience to come.
This could be the room
my body chose to grow in,
unaware of the fear that crept around my being
to spread its devilish cloak over my heart.
From this room I can pick at the bones of a story
and wonder at the hell of it,
when pain could be felt but never fathomed,
when adventure came with risk
and love, always a gamble.
But I can lie here in this room as I do now,
and warm my heart on the soft memory of youth,
with quiet in the air, and the lights of the night
gliding across my ceiling,
whilst all these wakeful musings seal my fate.

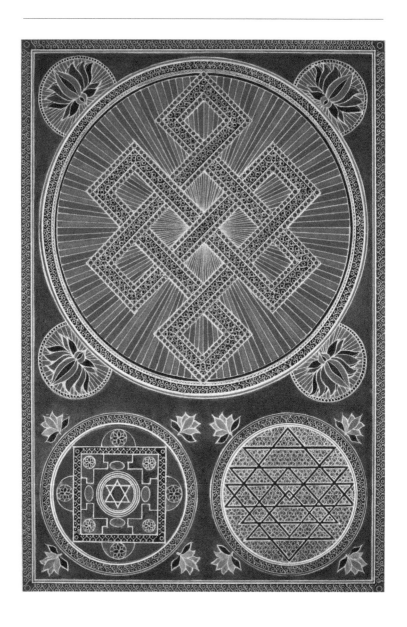

Suddenly I wept
at the horror of war;
the war of my childhood,
and the final twist of the knife
that till now only tickled my throat.
Now comes the rush of the blood
from the heart to the head,
and the eyes of a wounded man.
Death spills from the swirling carnage;
the perpetrators cheer in the tears and the blood
while the dying pierce the pungent air with their screams,
and the curled claws of the winged scavengers
tug on the limbs of children;
a crooked beak sunk deep into the flesh.
At home we call them brave,
praising these men
whilst choking on our lies,
looking for death in our heroes,
like the vulture looking for meat from their prey,
to glide on again to the next battlefield.
Suddenly I wept,
as the severed head of a last dead image
rolled to a halt in the bloodied gutter of my war.
I wept for the loss of the years
I had struggled to fill
with vain explanations.
I wept with the mothers of men like me,
and share in the grief for their long-lost cause,
and stand on the graves of their silent sons.

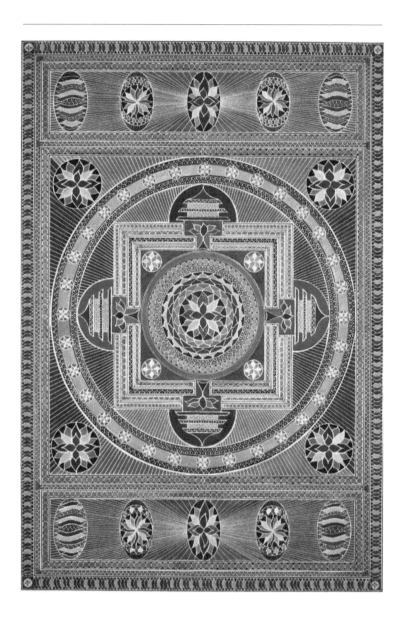

The silence now, betrays a chaos then.
The quiet night hangs exhausted on the air,
aching from life, resting in the gentle heaven,
no longer disguising its tired bones.
We survive in the darkness, free from oppression,
free from the pain we once endured.
We are bathed in still waters
where once we were tossed,
dried by the air once that would chill.
We return, are returned,
to reclaim our place on the land,
waiting for the day
without the urgency of youth.
No sound without, but a noisy past within.
Rest, where once there was effort.
We return in the silence to the innocence of then,
the taste of deluded hopes
still lingering on the lips.
And as I stand on this earth today in final surrender;
the same earth I struggled to defend,
seeking a purpose or looking for faith,
a long thin line of light
breaks through the night sky.
The warm dark silence
haunts those final days.

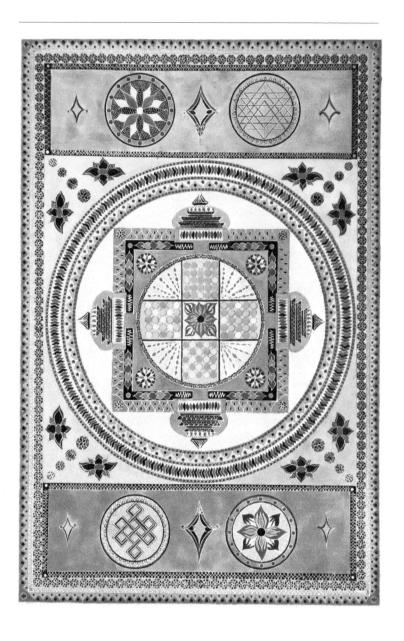

A stench of dusty fur;
the dried carcass of a long-gone rat
amongst the broken bricks
where once a family may have lived,
or children played, or a grandmother sewed.
We were now boy-ish soldiers
climbing those mounds of rubble
in search of spoils, or criminals,
or maybe war-heroes, or even dead cats.
We rummaged in moth-eaten settees,
in rooms with no floors, hanging on to railings,
looking down into our battlefield:
the bomb-site we called the dump.
These were the empty broken bottles of childhood,
discarded rugs, wet and smelly,
frayed cushions left by the dead,
or even the Germans themselves.
You didn't know it then
but it was death you could smell.
This was our own real-life war,
where we were the heroes
who'd always return home to the gas-fire,
and to cheese on toast at the end of our fighting day.
This was our climbing frame,
dust on our shoes from the bomb-strewn debris,
ruins on the corner of Cadogan Street and Draycott.
Through the smoke of our victories we rose,
gallant defenders, riding home
on invisible horseback,
blind to the truth that one day soon
we too would be lying
like rats in the ruins of a life-time battle,
soon maybe, really to die.

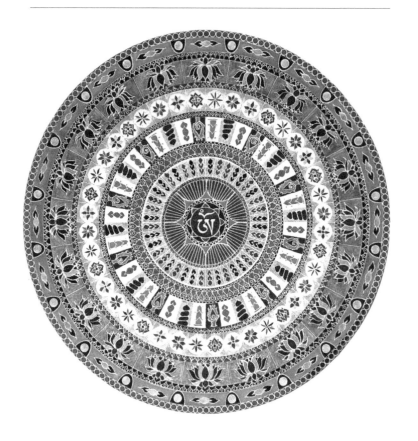

You my spirit, travel a pathless land where horizons fade;
your journey is unrecognized, existing in a timeless zone.
Your purpose is concealed;
though your shapeless presence remains;
you were conjured in defiance of this emptiness,
revealed in the silence of a void, you,
immeasurable force for the flowering of unheard sonnets;
you, the perpetrator, perfect in every blemish;
instinct chose you, drew strength from your every breath.
You came from within when I walked alone,
because that was your choice. and because horizons fade.
You live where these abstracts dissolve,
pin-sharp clarity in a desolate landscape.
This is where we meet, here in the occasional garden,
through fallacy and prophesy, one thought to the next;
you survey your pathless land on dry grit, cool granite,
in more than a handful of cities,
son and heir to the deluded vulture,
cloaked in cerebral disguise.
But you came in from the soul, not as a thought,
but as essence behind the word,
in response to my wasted whereabouts.
You are the vessel, the channel through whom,
belly to brain, all my power ebbs and flows.
You meander through my flesh, drifting beyond fantasy,
rebounding and resounding in all your many intervals.
Do I really need to describe the meaning of these images,
fleeting glimpses of harmony in my exquisite emptiness?
I have come too far with you to know.
You are part of my core, even when the vapors rise.
I have you in my blood, in all of my translations;
we are one behind the word, beyond all explanations.

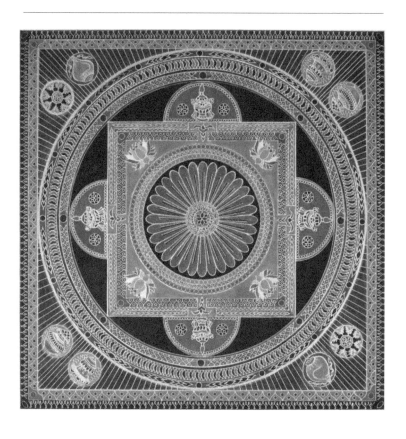

Where is the simple?
Is it here beyond the complex?
Is it in the negation of action,
reaction, emotion, thought, awareness;
beyond all this awareness?
This is the simple:
not as you have tried to explain,
not after, nor before,
not in this attention to detail;
ultimately unaware:
this is where simple lies.

And where is the silent?
Is it here behind the chatter?
Is it more than just quietness,
imagined whilst sleeping,
alert to all this,
and beyond meditation?
This is where silent is:
not in the absence of noise,
nor in resting,
but in being, not in doing;
in not even noticing;
ultimately not even this.
This is where silent is.

Silent and simple lie beyond our life and death,
not in time nor in entity, nor in the heart of these;
they are structured to our being, yet no part of us.
They are not a sleeping thing,
nor a thing that lies beyond chaos,
not a dull thing, nor easy to employ.
Silent, simple, are none of these.

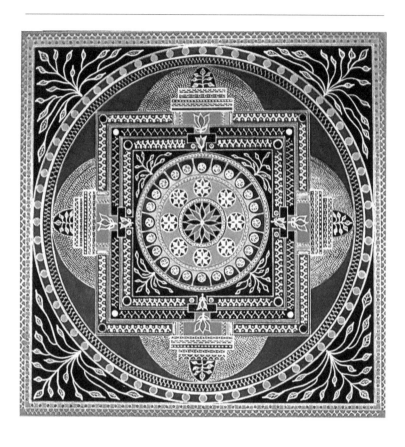

L et them ask the poets for the way.
We can only lie here
left to fumble and forge a sorry path.
Whatever is beyond us,
is beyond being;
being withers in the sanctity of our oasis;
being was conceived in the fear of losing,
construed by a paltry mind.
Mind is for the maintenance of suffering.
Out there, lies nothing
either imagined or imaginable.
so do not ask the scientist, or theist,
philosopher or seer.
Let the poets lead the way.
If these are only the ways of the mind,
the providence and possession of the gatherer,
the domain of those who take up a crown
to scramble to the summit of this pile of humankind,
then let us ask the poets to explain.
For mercy we will beg,
though the giver will not see,
and the tortured soul will not feel,
so the pain can cease to be.
Fearfully we'll scream,
in the wake of our sorrow:
a full-bellied roar
thundering through the corridors of memory.
Our many sided reasons,
excuses for immoral moments
nurtured in the poet's bosom,
will wither in the wind;
we have exchanged our emptiness
for platitudes, false promises of bliss,
and rigid imaginations of the future.

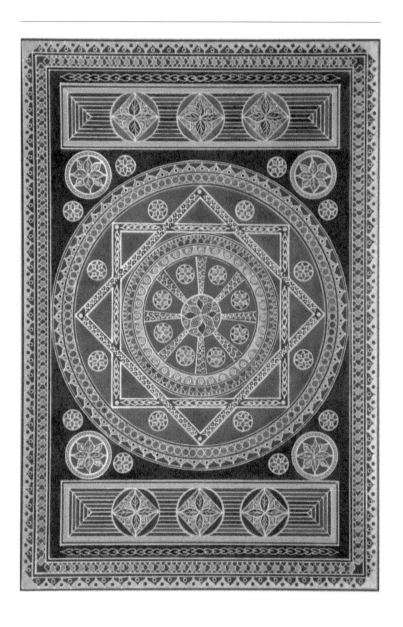

Your greed has left you hungry
for the want of a clean spirit;
You have lived in bitter condemnation;
sneered in the face of progress;
and denied the natural course.
Your foolish resistance to simplicity
gave you no hope of recompense.
You were insistent in your metaphors,
blinded by your arrogance,
and cornered in the remnants
of your artificial rooms.
This is your magnificat,
your final benediction;
this, your destination
in the face of just rewards.
Swallowed up by your own hunger;
this is your starvation
in the belly of your despair.

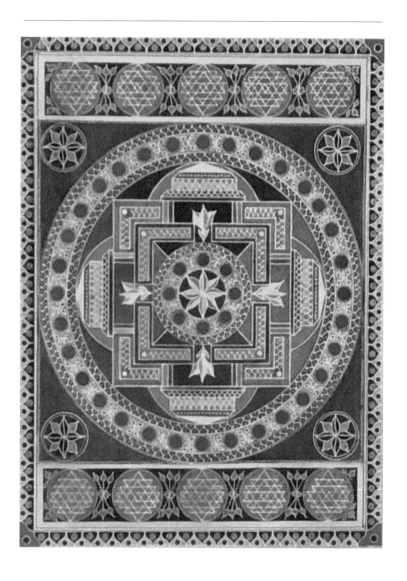

In clear skies
they ask me to define the wind.
The silence is broken
by the rustle of many leaves.
Offering them nothing,
I look up to the sky,
but they continue to philosophize
in aimless circles.

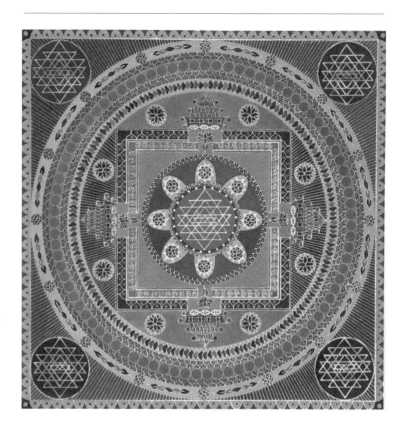

The past rolls from me like dust from a speeding train.
It left a sycamore naked, and rolls back down again
To the memories of youth, refined by my hidden pain.

The worst of what's remembered, my heart would not accept;
Denial was a duty; I was forever in its debt,
Repaying it with sorrow; it has not ended yet.

First I lived quite manfully, with scars that ran so deep;
Prepared to stomach hardship as long as I could keep
A single thread of beauty, to soothe me into sleep.

But soon my grip was loosened in the restless night ahead;
If the truth was ever told me, I rejected what was said;
I could only turn my eyes away, to live a dream instead.

There are no boundaries round the kingdom of a dream;
Whatever its reality, it's not what it may seem;
We build with no foundations; delusion reigns supreme.

Dreams fall to earth like dust from a speeding train,
Never to be gathered, never felt again.
The past was just a breeze I tried to harness. All in vain.

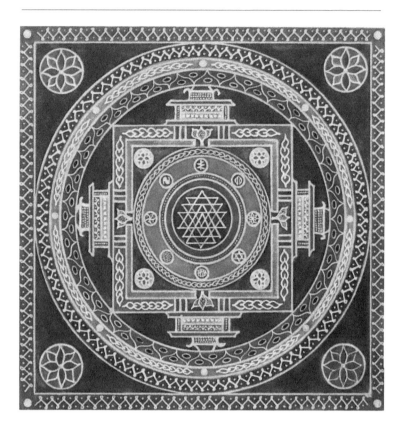

I heard you child, but did I heed you?
I carried you once, but did I free you?
I fed you then; do I still need to?
I heard you there, but child I didn't heed you.

I may have hurt you, but did I mean to?
And when I give, do I only seem to?
I felt you there; but do I still feel you?
I think I may have hurt you, but child I didn't mean to.

My heart cries out, but do you hear it?
I cry inside, but never fear it.
I'd give it all, and try to show it.
My heart is yours, and child you know it.

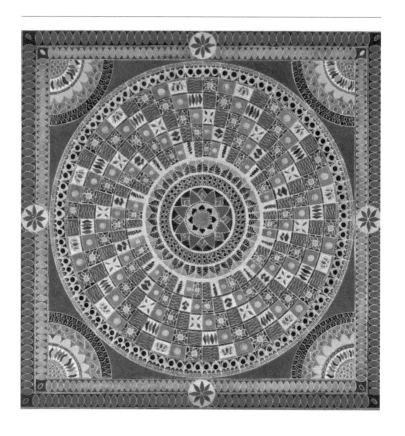

Should I look for life in a grain of sand,
discover death in spaces in between?
Should my eyes foresee or soul fore-tell?
Should memory translate or past reveal
those agonies carved out of my own frailty?

I am just a scavenger, dry-lipped with thirst,
chapped hands scratching in the dirt upon all fours.
Should my spirit feel, or heart still persevere?
Some would scoff, and some would turn away.
Most would make excuses, give explanations,
find interpretations to justify or blame.

All the while the grit's embedded deep
in the ball of foot or hand, or graze of knee;
it's only washed away by torment's relentless quest.
Self-appointed masters of the race,
purity ravaged by your greed and fear,
godliness withering in your churches,
you adorn your saints with images of piety and self-
      effacement,
as you procure and entrap your helpless prey.
Your fox-like cunning wreaks havoc,
intellect swollen with the spoils of your sacrifice,
your separate conscience grimacing in its tomb.

And I am at the centre of your storm,
part of the holocaust, framed with your nature.
I am both the victim and perpetrator,
oppressed by all that is angry in me.
Your folly is my reflection, mine is yours.
We both claim our inheritance,
spitting out the gristle as we chew.

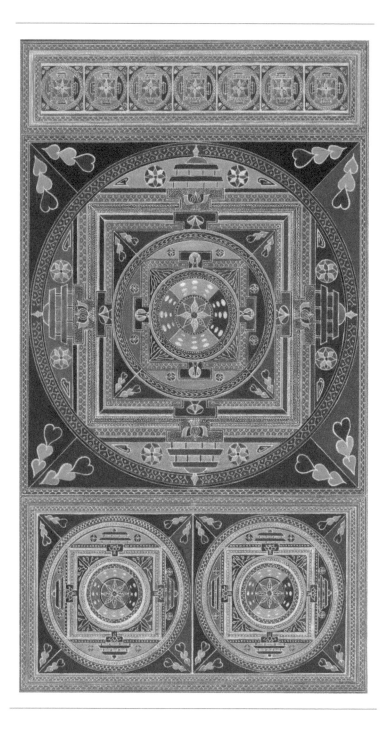

You have finally left me,
never to return again;
But it was me that walked away.
You weren't meant to go.
I meant for you to stay,
so that I could return one day.

Could you just for a moment,
stay there upon that spot;
and allow us to return again
to our dance of sacrifice and loss!

Let me walk away from you again,
then turn around, you begging me to stay,
so that I may choose you once again,
you still there, wanting me.

But you have finally left me,
and never to return again;
you have completely let me go.
I have lost you,
and the years
will bury
our love.

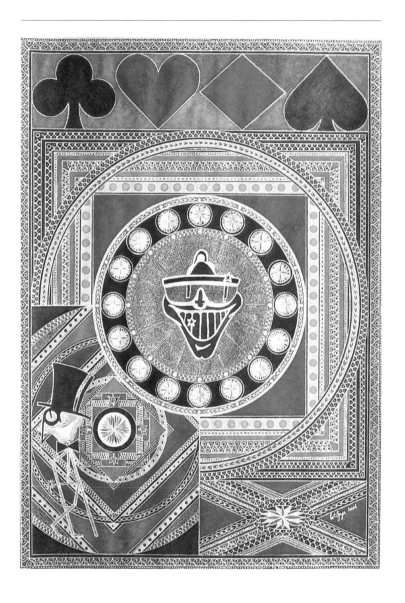

I saw my fire, I saw my pain.
In the instant I awoke.
I saw the rain disturb the flower,
feeding deserts in one stroke.
I shuddered in heaven's sigh,
its breath upon the window of my soul.
I carved the name "surrender" on my heart,
and I led the proud wolf from his lair.
I held him there while his kingdom crumbled
and new life shot through his fertile ruins.
I caught myself sighing,
in the corners of a faded garden.
I strained to catch my breath,
wrestling with a fear of what you may bring.
I walked alone in my waste-land,
while all that grew looked on in sad dismay.
Easier to walk in that arid place,
fingers all raw from clawing at the soil,
cracks upon my knuckles,
and pain worming its way quietly
into my hungry heart,
than to journey with another soul.
Easier for sorrow to burn my eyes
even as I watch the flowers in May.
My pen could well describe, yes,
but my heart could not convey.

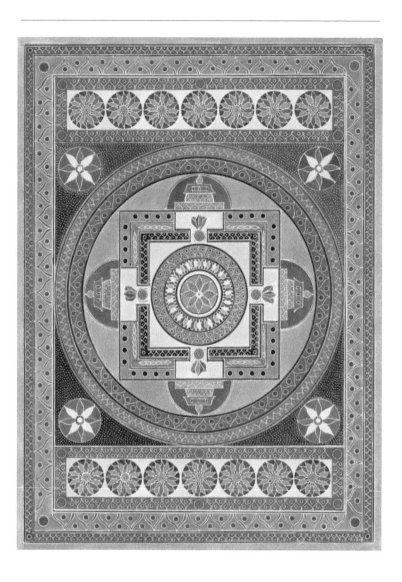

I would trade the past to which I cling
for just a moment pondering
beside this quiet lake.
The past is gone,
but I would trade it, all that I have known,
for just a moment here.
There were times I sometimes shared,
I lost so much in days of old,
and there are a thousand stories I have told.
And all my rambling thoughts and songs I wrote
are nothing but expressions that I quote.
But beside that quiet lake
there is the truest song to sing;
Now I look for the finest things.
I never knew what was in store;
what lies behind the mystery door.
And all my hopes and aspirations fade
beside the joy that has been made
beside this quiet and peaceful lake;
I am innocent and wise;
with a most blessed prize.

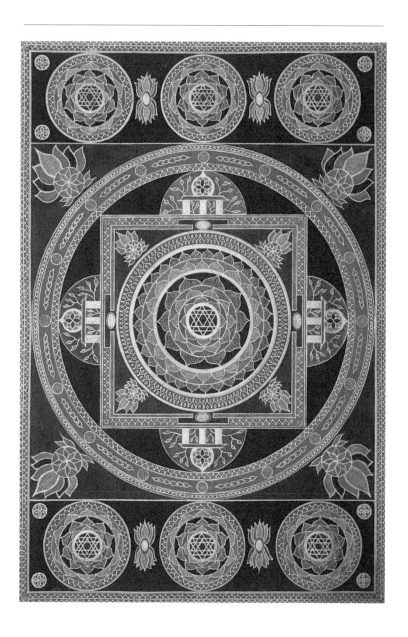

We two will meet in neutral places
where the heart cannot be torn;
we will drink alone from natural wells
whose water purifies the dawn;
dawn of life becoming,
flowing through our veins;
veins, these passages that feed
whatever still remains.
We will not own the moisture nor
the movement of a kiss;
we will have no right to own,
or even covet, bliss.
We can only watch as first
the river, then the stream,
carries from our hearts all that
we nurtured in a dream.
Meek and lowly,
I lie tonight in a space beyond your reach.
The soul repairs in silence
while the ashes of my sorrow
are scattered by the breath of the now,
woven in the stillness of no-mind;
born in the new next moment.

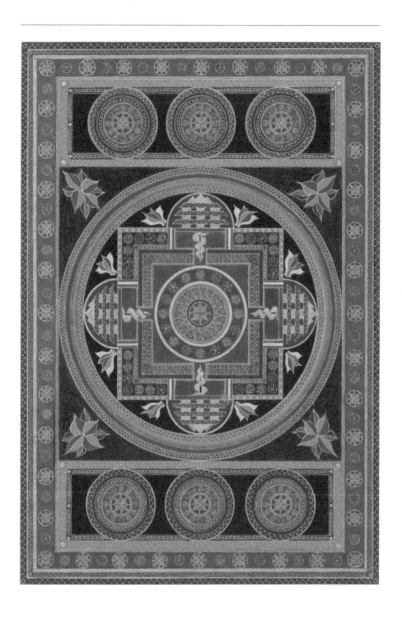

Should I tap into the source?
Plunge into its fertile soil at a random moment's notice?
Should I seek a stream of words that babble there
beneath the bridges I have crossed?
Maybe I'll find a soul there lurking
in the shadows of old rooms
where once I stored a consciousness
that guarenteed my words.
Scanning those hills and distant valleys today,
I burned to declare all they had set aflame within,
I longed for that sleeping spirit to rise
and stir up my senses again.
This reckless hand now carves the course
my instant thoughts had planned.
And here upon a single page,
it quells my longing to be heard
above the din of an impetuous self.
I now sit in the stillness of reflection,
the coveted jewel transformed
to glory by this glittering stream.
I am honouring my gracious muse.

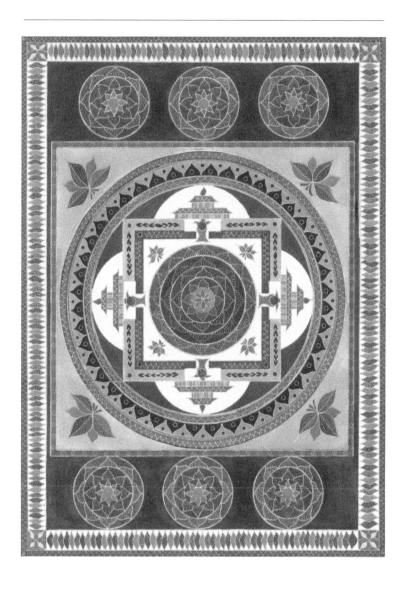

He lives in me
who failed to see
the light of foreign notions.
When he raised his eye,
his forbidding sky
looked down on his devotions.
Unintentional words poured forth
as heaven's utterings
came through the rays, the sun whose haze
was a flock of fledglings fluttering.
His eyes were squint and wet to touch,
his mouth was all a quiver.
He woke inside these late life lands,
and sailed on the wintry river.
He lives in me,
far from the days
when he was young and agile.
He bursts with joy
to recognize
his heart is still so fragile.
So full of song,
he comes along
to find his limbs all seeing.
This is where he started,
here to celebrate his being.

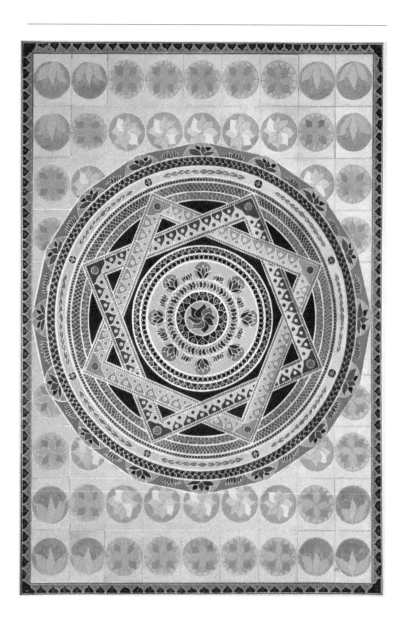

How quickly love
can turn to hate?
How soon these tight lips
have replaced the smouldering swell
of a lover's mouth.
How painful, love's balm,
when the tables turn,
with the fertile sap all
squeezed from the aching thigh.
Burning heart,
charred by love's seething counterpart,
fear no more the edge
of your passion's blade.
Take your pain with honour bestowed,
for you have not loved in vain.
Love had chosen you for a while;
you have been blessed by its passion;
passion that flowed through your chambers,
you the vehicle for its flight of glory,
never ending songstress,
harmonious song complete.
Fear no more love's journey;
new blood flows now through your veins,
bright as freedom, yours alone,
love's gift, unending.

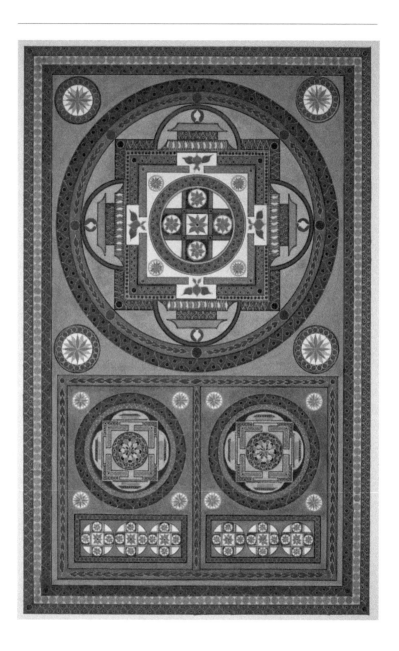

Now that I'm much older than you were when you died,
I can dare to hold you closer, dearer to my heart.
No more the desperation of my longing.
Now, I hold your memory and I cherish.
Untampered with by fantasies and needs,
my memory is a mirror,
revealing the touch of our friendship,
and the innocence of your beauty,
the true heart of the love you gave.
May that memory never distort over time,
but rather, let it reveal to me much more
than what I longed for in my grief.
Let the pure essence of you be alive in me today,
untouched by pain or even memory,
so that the truth of you will always live on,
and your spirit never die.

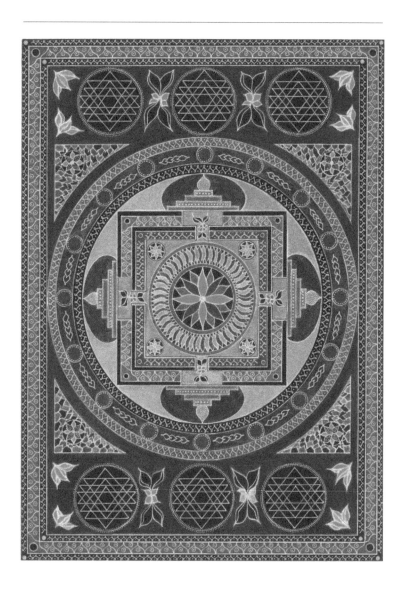

The deserter has made it,
avoiding all landmines;
crawling through his war-torn fields,
he is leaning at last against
the battlements of old fortresses,
coveting the truth while reality lingers,
while he craves an indulgence
that he learns to avoid.
Seeking refuge in prayer,
dissolving all reason to care
for the lonely old souls
left to be salvaged by scavenger priests
who lurk around altars looking for brethren.
Replenished and cleansed
by the innermost recess of instant recall,
his words become weapons
against once having been there,
lost in the material, and functioning blindly.
Last night the wolves in pursuit were the enemy;
now they are slaves to his need for expansion,
granting him succour and grist for the mill.
Once there were seasons imposed by misfortune,
a thousandfold reasons to die left unheeded.
Live on, say the souls who have followed on,
rejecting religion, savouring love.
They have surfaced from nightmares
and swim through his dreams,
though tomorrow was never more close and forboding,
He sweeps it away, riding horses of valkyrie;
all avenues trodden, at long last discarded,
the path becomes clear
for the day he can trust.

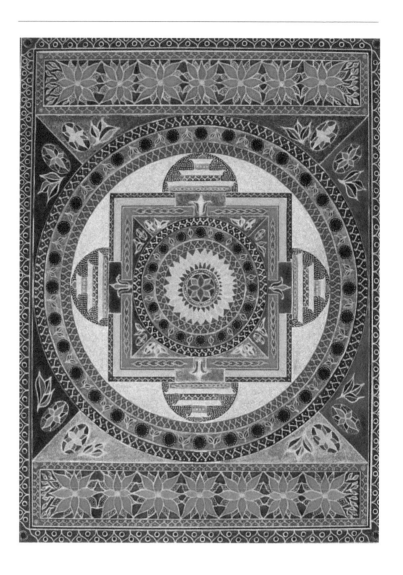

We labour to survive this mortal coil,
    but finally there comes relief.
Less to strive for, less for weary hands to hold.
I'd seek a reason for it all if I didn't already know why.
The flame is now a waning ember.
Fear and loss drive me, clamouring on my journey.
Living by the rules, still I side-step all the traps.
Often we'd use them as a muse,
to avoid their consuming animal,
always just one step ahead.
Standfast, we were told, all hope fading;
standfast, they'd say, let reason go.
If our eyes were clear to see with,
then surely they'd have known
how our tears conspired to cloud them.
If my heart were more than muscle,
most surely it would ache
with this dead-weight body down below
that moves, but cannot feel.
When it stirs it's only flesh surviving,
or bones shuddering in their gristle,
their water daring the skin to quake,
cool on the dry surface of my flesh.

This body no longer feeds like it did;
its sinews contract without compassion.
I'd seek a reason it should die if I didn't already know.
In a darkened corner, sometimes I cower in secret,
holding the reins and remnants of my fear.
I count the passing seconds until my memory fails,
peering into strange caves with mouldy walls
and holy sinners, awaiting transformation,
not knowing just quite when.

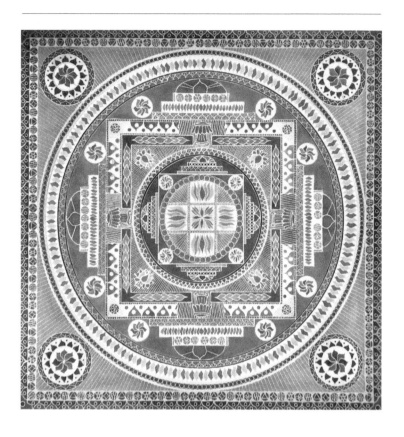

This is a time for reflection,
not tears.
The honeysuckle in July
harmlessly waits to talk
of the long dark season's rest
just past,
when winter winds
rocked the fences,
and roads to our relatives
were blocked
or waterlogged,
saturating homes,
as we nervously
waited indoors.
The pigeon in the eaves
coos like a dove today;
there's a distant splash
and gleeful cries
of a child in a garden pool
colouring the simmering
summer air.

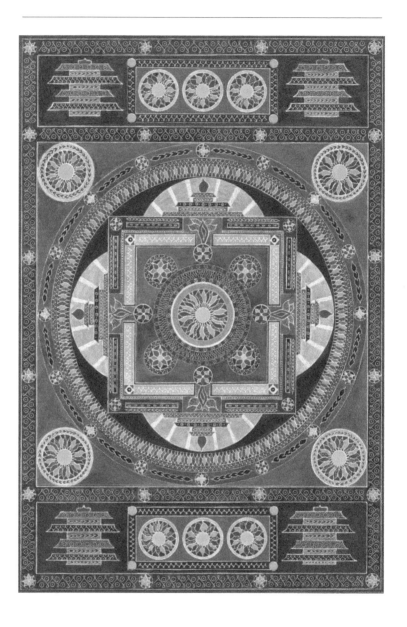

I hear my mother's voice
in the distant forest of experience:
she tells me to forgive myself,
whilst the ones I love move on.

There's a heat today
that I recognise from once before,
when walking in sandals,
with the voice of my sister in my ear,
reminding me of our mother's decline.
She left too soon to find release
from the pain and heartache she endured.
But now, she was free,
telling me "yes, here on earth we suffer,
and that beyond
lies our freedom from that suffering".

Mother of all my views and aspirations,
you cleanse me now.
I never thought I would reach you again,
never to tell you how much you meant.
But now I can say farewell, dear mother,
here in the shade of my peaceful age.
I just came to catch you in the fleeting breeze
that teased me away from this stifling heat.

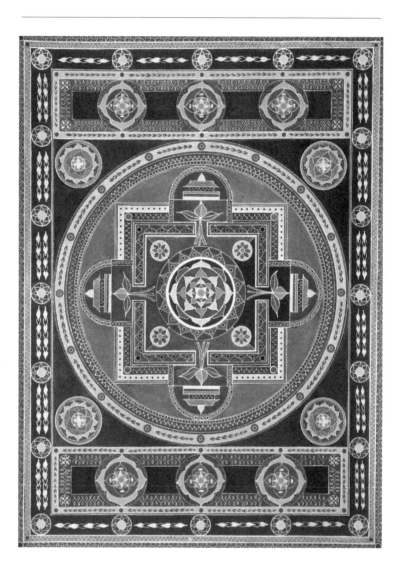

Peace, my haven,
  butterflies and bees,
Cley Hill calls me, easy.
Paths I never trod before,
the world in a pebble,
palm of the hand,
journey's endlessness, within.
Steep meanderings take me, boundless, unbound.
Clouds, like mobiles dangling in the sky,
still like the air.
Summer's aroma slowly moving;
like clouds.
Breeze like breath, untasted yet.
Tears now stifled by pain unmet.
On to heights by rugged paths
encircling Cley some thousand since.
May I not this Cley bequeath
to all who walked here,
whose loves now leave?
Or do I step to my fate's own beat,
alone around these paths where lovers meet?
Alone, with the lazy heat around my neck,
and these, my unsteady feet.
On to heights of turf and clay,
wind-beaten shrub now at play.
Dare I trudge where cattle graze,
all dark and brown whose offspring gaze
on my aching heart now out of phase?
Peace comes to Cley.
The sound of time past,
now muffled by this present.
Perfection unrecognisable
in this, the purest of moments.

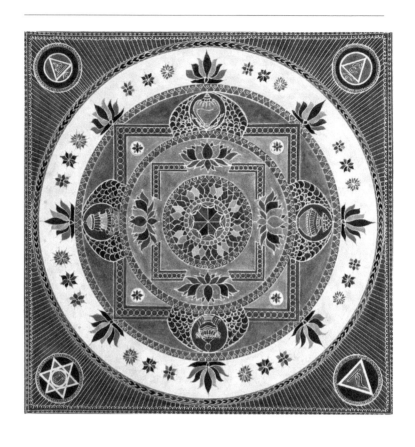

For a moment we were children.
Every word we spoke was gold.
Our voices faltered as we parted.
You said we would meet again some day.
I said yes, believing no.
You, fully fledged, your own woman.
I, your real father,
my view of you
still held in a handful of snapshots,
from the aching pain of our loss,
to your re-birth
and your final independence.

In those last few seconds together,
each word we spoke was golden;
in each silence so much was said,
we two, father and child,
immersed as one in our old familiar grief.
Just for a while, our last hug lingered on.
Neither would we surrender.
We were one.
A one-ness that choked us in those final moments,
and brought us back to the day.

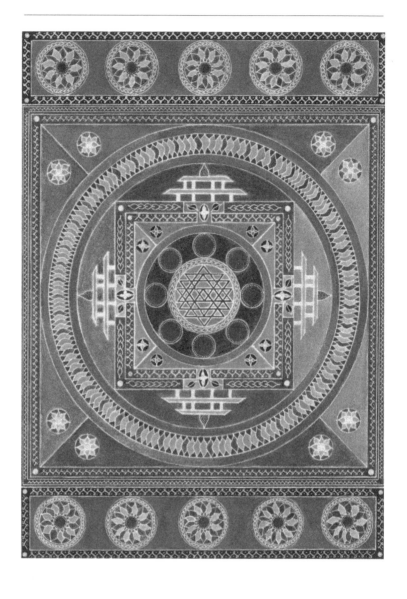

I sat in the blazing heat watching
the shimmering silhouettes,
faces in a haze wearing
all the hopelessness of this age.
These souls broke into thoughts
of my coastal bliss long past;
they trampled through my contemplation,
gentle respite from the world.
But in these faces I saw the remnants
of my own blank past;
lost to a cold existence,
my soul drained of hope.
Though now I gaze through the rays of an unforgiving sun,
nurturing my long lost child,
all distant and detached, and reckless as a butterfly,
in these faces I saw my old sorrow, burning
on the sun-drenched ground at my feet.

My voice stays quiet
and my heart beats slowly,
nothing is forced, for my time is now;
the past is over; done forever
and I weep no more for tomorrow.
I welcome my hand being pulled by a child,
the other returning me home
to the heaven I found hope in,
a room where I was born,
this canny place
where the sins of my fathers
leave no stains upon
the virtues of their sons.

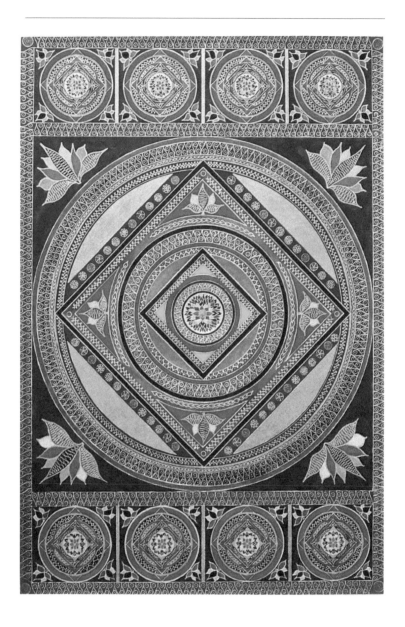

Respectable avoidance, acceptable lies.
Though we ought,
I fear we never will
confront this masquerade,
this mockery of truth
that sidles in the corners
of our consciousness.

Too engaged are we
with the laying down of laws.
We construct convenient
passageways of escape,
acting out on our fear
of the emptiness.

Thus we survive,
damaged along the way,
to justify and reason with existence,
to swerve round love
when it causes pain,
but to gather its fruit
for its sensual gain.

We've lost the beauty of the night;
the darkness in the soul masks it all;
so much more to reveal
should we dare
to strip away, repair,
pretence, and false self.
Only our politeness remains;
smothering our connections,
and glorifying respectability.

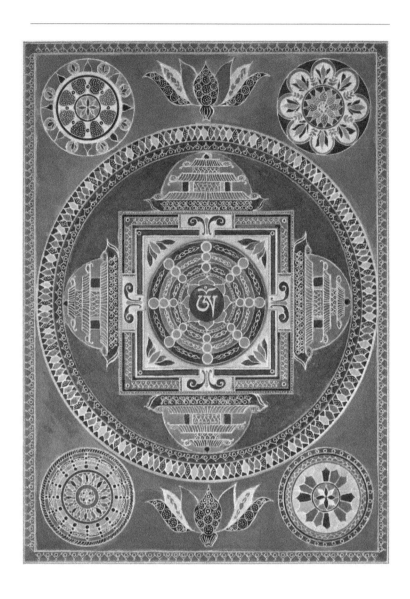

How is it now in heaven, my love;
how is our heaven on earth?
Do you still radiate warmth
as once you used to do?
If your heart can now trust love,
do you leave its fate to the the gods,
in faith it will remain eternal?
I can only observe our heaven;
no more describe the ways of its truth
than I can the purpose of my soul.
But as we wander through these reveries,
are we not more than just two souls
with differences between us?

How is it for you in heaven, love?
How is our heaven on earth?
I'm still here in restful surrender,
without conclusion;
stripped of my senses;
blind to this light,
and deafened by what
could have been angels singing,
penetrating each fibre of my being.

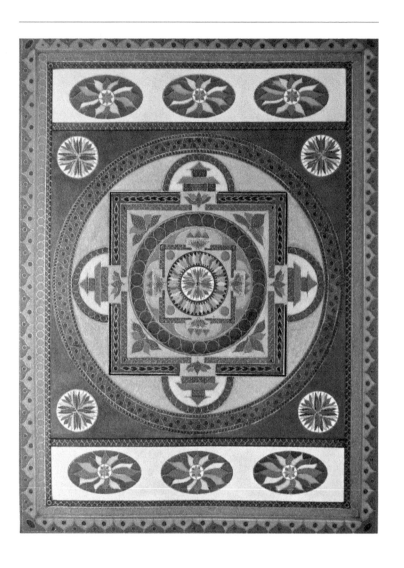

Certain of us floundered as other mortals died;
we who lost our way sometimes had justice on our side;
not the kind of justice measured by the law,
but a universal harmony, untouched, and from the core.

Those whose lives were ended, burned out,
though not in vain,
were granted immortality, were spared unchartered pain.
But we who stayed by choice or not,
were left sometimes alone
to gain insight through circumstance,
as wise men once had done.

The memory, the martyrdom, of the ever sacred dead
was glorified in heavenly words just like the poet said,
whilst we, who grieve their loss of life,
hold on to the last strands
of hope that we will one day come to fully understand

that which never we have known, which never can be felt,
which lies beyond time's grip,
before our fateful hand was dealt.
Finally we floundered where the others must have died;
sometimes we found acceptance, and harmony inside.

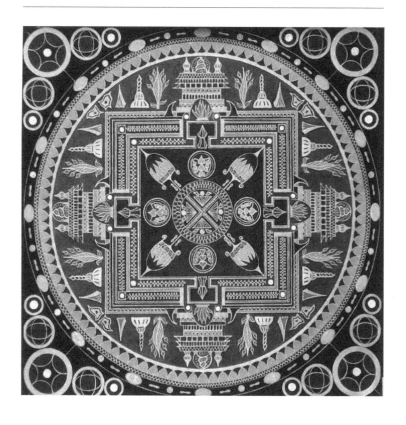

Things;
    just things remain.
Here on the dresser, there up the stairs,
packed in boxes,
in first this,
then the other cupboard,
relics of the days we try not to forget,
gathering dust, where once
they shone so brightly.
In worlds we invented
varying moods of a world,
where we scrambled around
searching for a purpose
beyond the one we know.
Days long gone,
many days past,
just one after the other,
remembered days encompassed in things;
things gathering dust upon the dresser,
with long ago books now yellowing,
that will never be read again.
Standing back from it all,
still it remains:
no purpose;
no reason to search for a purpose,
ever spiralling,
in descending circles
with a weariness
that leaves me speechless.

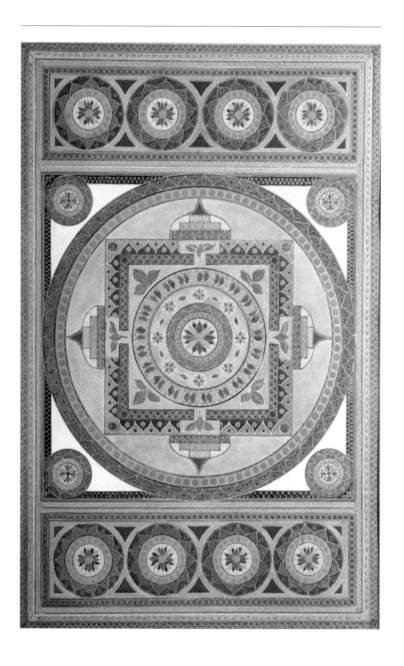

That sad moment you stuck by your word
and told me we must part;
the hole you left for me to fill
with solitude, or art.
I tried to say how cruel you were,
to make you feel remorse.
I wanted you to feel some pain,
and to take me back, of course.

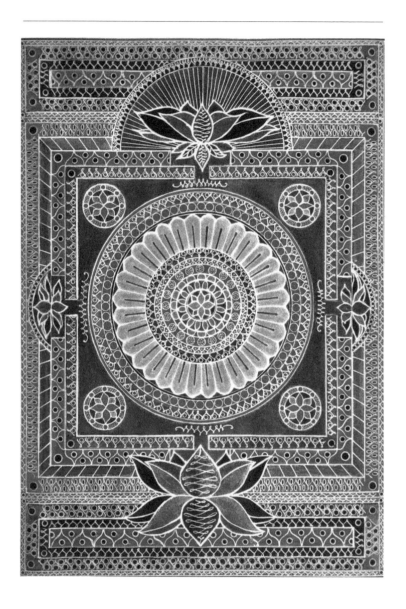

Reflecting here like a wise old cat,
with neither disdain nor a smile.
The days of fight for survival are over.
The still mind has dissolved to nothing,
clearing the path, not to a ministerial heaven,
but to an imagined bliss,
with freedom from thought
that leaves me now, to see.
Wily old soldiers parade on their patch
like conquerors of old
returning from battle in their silence.
And the young bucks show their power as they play.
There's tangible energy in the air,
an excitement that glistens and inspires.
There's confidence on the wing,
unrecognised by human eye,
sitting here in this hide,
lost for words, and glad to be so;
for words invent no reverie
for the language of the soul.

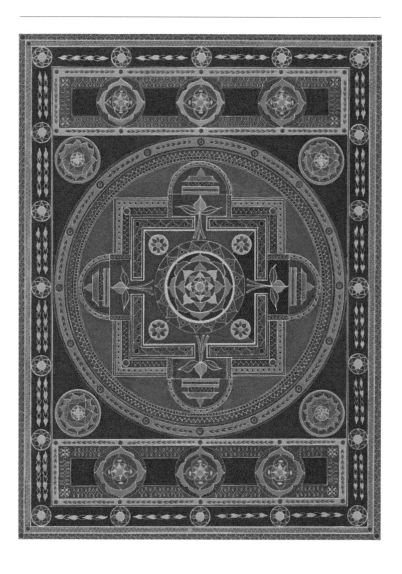

When you went away, a part of me died.
Though I stood strong in the dust and the rubble,
still I am bemused, not understanding your death.

Your soft voice says
"There's a place for you; you must believe it"
But I need you here to tell me
where or when to leave?
I can't hear you bid me walk
on your enchanted way.
"No matter, I'm still with you;
it's too soon for you to stray.
There's no need to fear.
Mine is the same fate of others
you loved who now have passed away"
I remember how I asked you once
what is it holds us near?
What you told me when I turned,
forever I'll hold dear.
"My friend", you said,
"what will bind us in my passing
is the love we offer now,
here,
on earth,
to each other,
as much as our hearts allow"

Now your life is gone my friend;
the love you spoke of then
is the love I carry now;
I wonder does that part of me
that died with you
live on in your holy death?

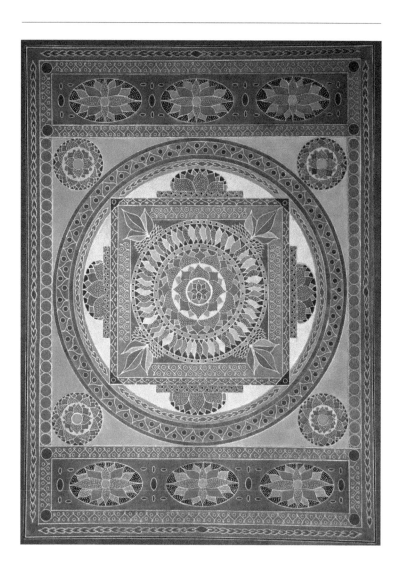

In a moment of surrender,
I want to shed a tear,
to live peacefully not knowing
what lies beyond the senses;
I yearn for the rush of abandonment
in an instance of ecstasy;
all these freedoms were smothered long ago
in the agony of all my losses.

So what is there to praise?
The bells that rang for freedom
are now stifled by conflict and dying;
children crushed by greed and neglect,
even lying in ditches with the oil of predatory guns
still gleaming in their innocent blood;
the moan and the murmur of sustained grief
echos with the constant chorus
of those who are out to win,
their humility smothered by acquisition,
their modesty discredited by derision and mockery,
their rapture denigrated by the chains of achievement.
Little is left of innocence,
save the one true journey within;
freedom lies somewhere
in my sobbing heart;
in loss and resignation of
all we've left undone.

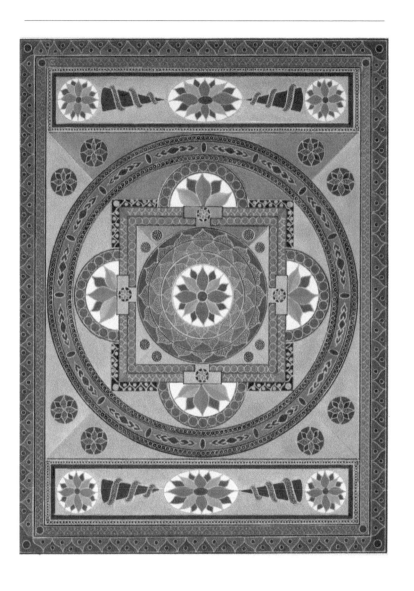

Have I ever told you of my love for sunny Somerset?
Blue skies in January, when it's not even warm yet?
Green against the blue, and fields all wintry brown,
Nothing in the distance, the earth a solid ground?

I walked the lanes of Somerset that I dreamed of as a boy,
Though fantasies I had back then are nothing to the joy
I felt right here, a lifetime on, in this place I came to find
As I followed in the steps that I once took all in my mind.

I walked the fields of Somerset,on this shining January day
Before the Spring had broken, before the birds can say
That winter now is over, and frosts are not around,
But only budding crocuses by hedgerows can be found.

Though I grew up with concrete walls in cities as a child,
We often made our trips away to the country and the wild.
But I never knew the peacefulness, green fields all around,
As in this place I call my home, far from my old home town.

By the sunny fields of Somerset I walk my solitary way;
Beneath the skies where nature lies all throughout the day.
The day in fields of Somerset is forever mine to keep
Until that time it comes to pass that I may fall asleep.

No greater love have I today than for the path I took,
Though I didn't travel easily, and at times I dared not look;
But I am ever grateful now for that path as I stand here
Among the fields of Somerset that always feel so near.

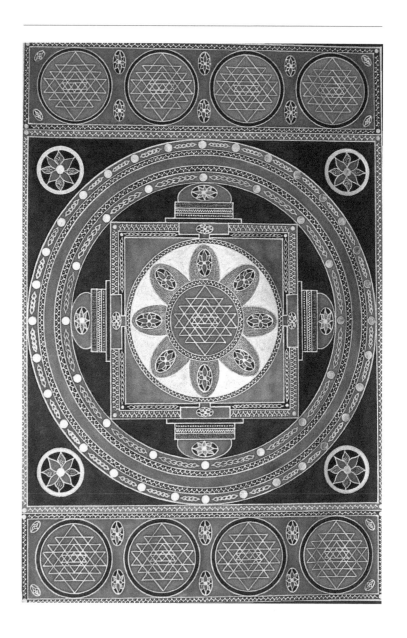

I'd carry myself upright walking into the wind.
I'd be glad in wool and mittens,
matching scarf and ruddy cheeked
down greenfield grasslands to the shore,
where rock and shingle meet with moss and thistle,
heather and gorse,
sodden paths beneath my feet,
untrampled upon since summer's over.
I'd be lord of this kingdom,
my body alive to nature's call,
natural call, thought-free and mild-mannered.
I'd live in trees and fly like the heron across those low lands,
returning to my love when the work was done,
silently perched in proud protection of my young.
I'd put the food that I'd gathered
into the nests of the needy,
and leave unnoticed,
the uninvited but welcome visitor,
I, father, seeking neither praise nor gratitude,
soaring as I patrol my acres,
fulfilling my dream, my never ending flight,
sleek invader,
with stories forever untold.

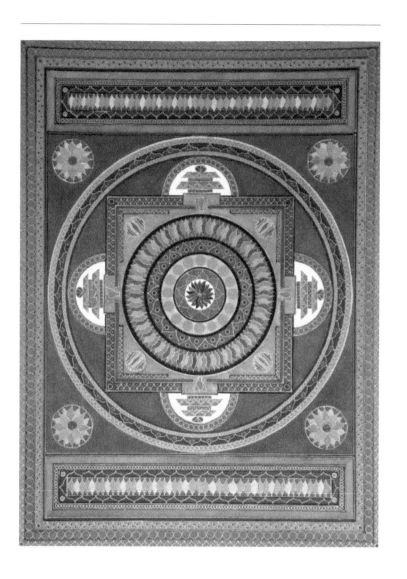

In clouds, there's light and shade.
White and grey.
Shapes of figures once known;
never forgotten, always remembered,
though sometimes not always re-called.
She has become like a mirror,
we two reflected in each the other's story.
The to-ing and fro-ing of our ideas,
snippets of conversation like those clouds,
they're enough to register our rapport,
just like in the wild they do,
those she-wolves and their mates,
understanding, unmeasured,
connection unrecognised
but securely framed in each moment
in the blinking of an eye.
How did we ever come to love like this,
without a smile, without a kiss,
you and I, never forgotten,
but often not always recalled.

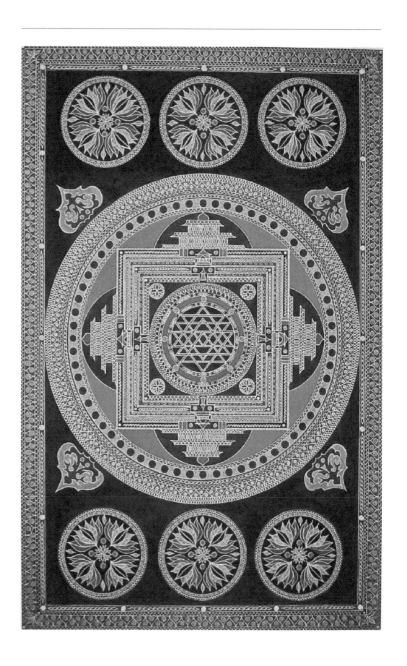

Once I may have sung
with raw voice, all gravel,
and lived in;
I walked through freezing silence,
hail and storm;
tall, and armed with bravado
that no-one dare deride.
But inside I was always small;
I feared the loss of my paltry attributes,
as I pushed them to the fore.

These days I tend to stumble;
I sing with cracked voice and roughness,
the inevitable end to a darkness I let enter
that at last no longer ignore.

Though once I walked
with my back all straight,
my legs now ache,
buckled from the weight
of time's ravage;
though my soul is bright,
I can sense its fading light.

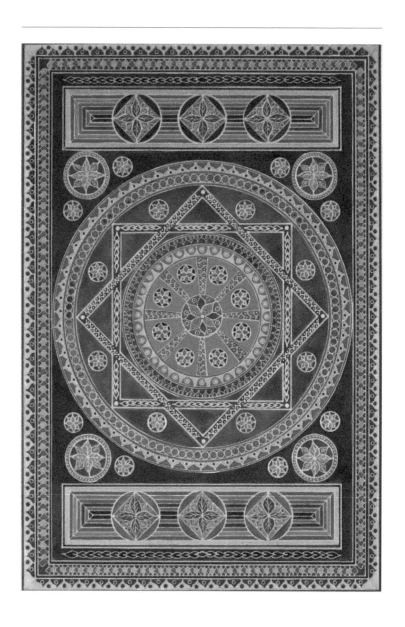

Tempted by this,
  tempted no more;
by that, nor the other;
all left behind;
tempted by nothing,
to rise again; to fly.

Tired of this?
Tired no more.
No wish to dream; only to be;
no more to score,
counting reason or possession;
stripped bare, face clear of line.

Clear of line; not in line.
Skirting the edges.
Avoiding the cracks,
whilst free to falter.
Blessed at the end
with gifts from the start;
gifts I kept in the story.

Ingram Content Group UK Ltd.
Milton Keynes UK
UKHW050803100523
421508UK00012B/169